Welcome!

If you're reading this, that means you completed step one of "UNLOCKING YOUR PURPOSE AND LETTING IT FUEL YOUR PASSION" aka the PFP workbook. Yay! I'm proud of you for realizing you needed help unlocking your purpose, taking the time out to complete the exercises in your workbook and now taking the time to sit with yourself & journal your thoughts. Remember in order to unlock your purpose you must be willing to live in your truth. This journal is to help you spend time alone and reconnect with yourself, while starting your journey in walking and living in your purpose. Writing is powerful! Writing is selfcare! Writing is personal! So, for the next 30 use this journal to write down your thoughts and feelings. Use it to help you gain self-knowledge, awareness and show you a purpose filled life worth living.

WHILE JOURNALING:

1. Find a place where you can be alone
2. Sit in silence
3. Find your favorite playlist on your phone, put your headphones in and press play! *if you said NO to #2*
4. Be intentional
5. Let the pen flow
6. Repeat steps 1-5 everyday
7. Keep writing take breaks if needed but NEVER stop writing
8. After day 30, find time to read everything you've written in your journal. Reflect on where you started to where you are now. GROWTH, UNDERSTANDING and DEVELOPMENT.

-Purp

"Live Life with a Purpose"

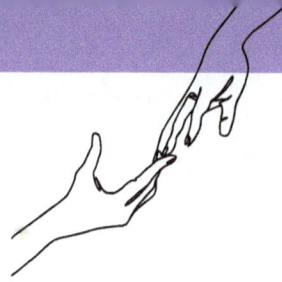

Morning Thoughts

Date: _____

Today I want to feel...

_____

_____

_____

Today I will spread kindness by...

_____

_____

_____

3 things I'm grateful for today are...

_____

_____

_____

"Happiness is a habit."

Evening Thoughts

3 things I'm grateful for today are...

_____

_____

_____

The best part of today was...

_____

_____

_____

What can I learn from today's experiences?

_____

_____

_____

Tomorrow I'm looking forward to...

_____

_____

_____

"Do more of what you love."

Things I'm proud of achieving today are...

_____

_____

_____

_____

_____

_____

_____

_____

_____

_____

_____

_____

_____

_____

"Believe. You're halfway there."

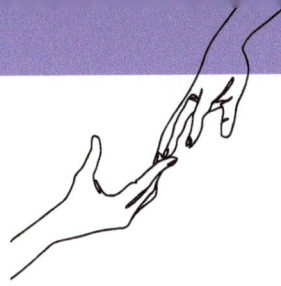

Morning Thoughts

Date: _____

Today I want to feel...

_____

_____

_____

Today I will spread kindness by...

_____

_____

_____

3 things I'm grateful for today are...

_____

_____

_____

"Happiness is a habit."

Evening Thoughts

3 things I'm grateful for today are...

_____

_____

_____

The best part of today was...

_____

_____

_____

What can I learn from today's experiences?

_____

_____

_____

Tomorrow I'm looking forward to...

_____

_____

_____

"Do more of what you love."

Things I'm proud of achieving today are...

_____

_____

_____

_____

_____

_____

_____

_____

_____

_____

_____

_____

_____

_____

"Believe. You're halfway there."

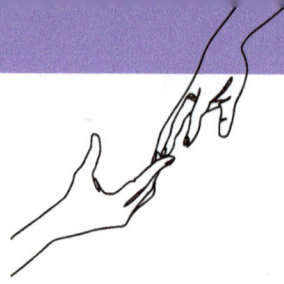

Morning Thoughts

Date: _____

Today I want to feel...

_____

_____

_____

Today I will spread kindness by...

_____

_____

_____

3 things I'm grateful for today are...

_____

_____

_____

"Happiness is a habit."

Evening Thoughts

3 things I'm grateful for today are...

_____

_____

_____

The best part of today was...

_____

_____

_____

What can I learn from today's experiences?

_____

_____

_____

Tomorrow I'm looking forward to...

_____

_____

_____

"Do more of what you love."

Things I'm proud of achieving today are...

_____

_____

_____

_____

_____

_____

_____

_____

_____

_____

_____

_____

_____

"Believe. You're halfway there."

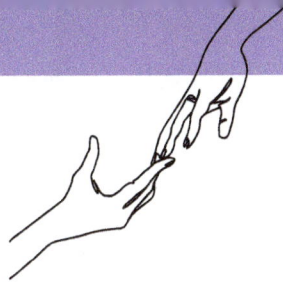

Morning Thoughts

Date: _____

Today I want to feel...

_____

_____

_____

Today I will spread kindness by...

_____

_____

_____

3 things I'm grateful for today are...

_____

_____

_____

"Happiness is a habit."

Evening Thoughts

3 things I'm grateful for today are...

_____

_____

_____

The best part of today was...

_____

_____

_____

What can I learn from today's experiences?

_____

_____

_____

Tomorrow I'm looking forward to...

_____

_____

_____

"Do more of what you love."

Things I'm proud of achieving today are...

_____

_____

_____

_____

_____

_____

_____

_____

_____

_____

_____

_____

_____

_____

"Believe. You're halfway there."

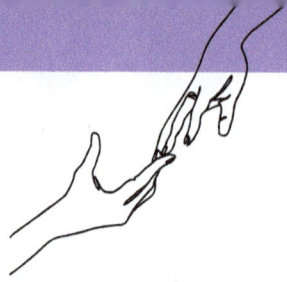

Morning Thoughts

Date: _____

Today I want to feel...

_____

_____

_____

Today I will spread kindness by...

_____

_____

_____

3 things I'm grateful for today are...

_____

_____

_____

"Happiness is a habit."

Evening Thoughts

3 things I'm grateful for today are...

_____

_____

_____

The best part of today was...

_____

_____

_____

What can I learn from today's experiences?

_____

_____

_____

Tomorrow I'm looking forward to...

_____

_____

_____

"Do more of what you love."

Things I'm proud of achieving today are...

_____

_____

_____

_____

_____

_____

_____

_____

_____

_____

_____

_____

_____

_____

_____

"Believe. You're halfway there."

Morning Thoughts

Date: _____

Today I want to feel...

_____

_____

_____

Today I will spread kindness by...

_____

_____

_____

3 things I'm grateful for today are...

_____

_____

_____

"Happiness is a habit."

Evening Thoughts

3 things I'm grateful for today are...

_____

_____

_____

The best part of today was...

_____

_____

_____

What can I learn from today's experiences?

_____

_____

_____

Tomorrow I'm looking forward to...

_____

_____

_____

"Do more of what you love."

Things I'm proud of achieving today are...

_____

_____

_____

_____

_____

_____

_____

_____

_____

_____

_____

_____

_____

"Believe. You're halfway there."

Morning Thoughts

Date: _____

Today I want to feel...

_____
_____
_____

Today I will spread kindness by...

_____
_____
_____

3 things I'm grateful for today are...

_____
_____
_____

"Happiness is a habit."

Evening Thoughts

3 things I'm grateful for today are...

_____

_____

_____

The best part of today was...

_____

_____

_____

What can I learn from today's experiences?

_____

_____

_____

Tomorrow I'm looking forward to...

_____

_____

_____

"Do more of what you love."

Things I'm proud of achieving today are...

_____

_____

_____

_____

_____

_____

_____

_____

_____

_____

_____

_____

_____

_____

_____

"Believe. You're halfway there."

Morning Thoughts

Date: _____

Today I want to feel...

_____

_____

_____

Today I will spread kindness by...

_____

_____

_____

3 things I'm grateful for today are...

_____

_____

_____

"Happiness is a habit."

Evening Thoughts

3 things I'm grateful for today are...

_____

_____

_____

The best part of today was...

_____

_____

_____

What can I learn from today's experiences?

_____

_____

_____

Tomorrow I'm looking forward to...

_____

_____

_____

"Do more of what you love."

Things I'm proud of achieving today are...

_____

_____

_____

_____

_____

_____

_____

_____

_____

_____

_____

_____

_____

_____

"Believe. You're halfway there."

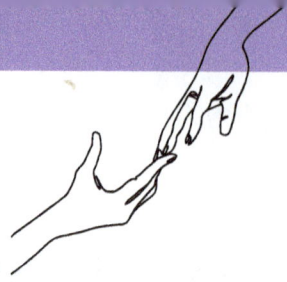

Morning Thoughts

Date: _____

Today I want to feel...

_____

_____

_____

Today I will spread kindness by...

_____

_____

_____

3 things I'm grateful for today are...

_____

_____

_____

"Happiness is a habit."

Evening Thoughts

3 things I'm grateful for today are...

_____

_____

_____

The best part of today was...

_____

_____

_____

What can I learn from today's experiences?

_____

_____

_____

Tomorrow I'm looking forward to...

_____

_____

_____

"Do more of what you love."

Things I'm proud of achieving today are...

_____

_____

_____

_____

_____

_____

_____

_____

_____

_____

_____

_____

_____

_____

_____

_____

"Believe. You're halfway there."

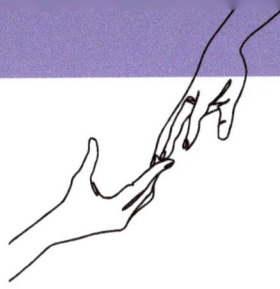

Morning Thoughts

Date: _____

Today I want to feel...

_____

_____

_____

Today I will spread kindness by...

_____

_____

_____

3 things I'm grateful for today are...

_____

_____

_____

"Happiness is a habit."

Evening Thoughts

3 things I'm grateful for today are...

_____

_____

_____

The best part of today was...

_____

_____

_____

What can I learn from today's experiences?

_____

_____

_____

Tomorrow I'm looking forward to...

_____

_____

_____

"Do more of what you love."

Things I'm proud of achieving today are...

_____

_____

_____

_____

_____

_____

_____

_____

_____

_____

_____

_____

_____

_____

"Believe. You're halfway there."

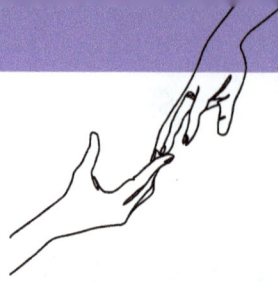

Morning Thoughts

Date: _____

Today I want to feel...

_____

_____

_____

Today I will spread kindness by...

_____

_____

_____

3 things I'm grateful for today are...

_____

_____

_____

"Happiness is a habit."

Evening Thoughts

3 things I'm grateful for today are...

_____

_____

_____

The best part of today was...

_____

_____

_____

What can I learn from today's experiences?

_____

_____

_____

Tomorrow I'm looking forward to...

_____

_____

_____

"Do more of what you love."

Things I'm proud of achieving today are...

_____

_____

_____

_____

_____

_____

_____

_____

_____

_____

_____

_____

_____

_____

"Believe. You're halfway there."

Morning Thoughts

Date: _____

Today I want to feel...

_____

_____

_____

Today I will spread kindness by...

_____

_____

_____

3 things I'm grateful for today are...

_____

_____

_____

"Happiness is a habit."

Evening Thoughts

3 things I'm grateful for today are...

_____

_____

_____

The best part of today was...

_____

_____

_____

What can I learn from today's experiences?

_____

_____

_____

Tomorrow I'm looking forward to...

_____

_____

_____

"Do more of what you love."

Things I'm proud of achieving today are...

_____

_____

_____

_____

_____

_____

_____

_____

_____

_____

_____

_____

_____

_____

_____

"Believe. You're halfway there."

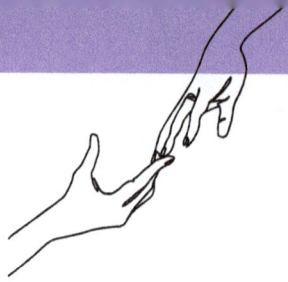

Morning Thoughts

Date: _____

Today I want to feel...

_____
_____
_____

Today I will spread kindness by...

_____
_____
_____

3 things I'm grateful for today are...

_____
_____
_____

"Happiness is a habit."

Evening Thoughts

3 things I'm grateful for today are...

_____

_____

_____

The best part of today was...

_____

_____

_____

What can I learn from today's experiences?

_____

_____

_____

Tomorrow I'm looking forward to...

_____

_____

_____

"Do more of what you love."

Things I'm proud of achieving today are...

_____

_____

_____

_____

_____

_____

_____

_____

_____

_____

_____

_____

_____

_____

"Believe. You're halfway there."

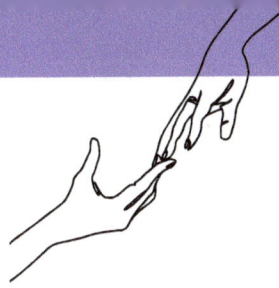

Morning Thoughts

Date: _____

Today I want to feel...

_____

_____

_____

Today I will spread kindness by...

_____

_____

_____

3 things I'm grateful for today are...

_____

_____

_____

"Happiness is a habit."

Evening Thoughts

3 things I'm grateful for today are...

_____

_____

_____

The best part of today was...

_____

_____

_____

What can I learn from today's experiences?

_____

_____

_____

Tomorrow I'm looking forward to...

_____

_____

_____

"Do more of what you love."

Things I'm proud of achieving today are...

_____

_____

_____

_____

_____

_____

_____

_____

_____

_____

_____

_____

_____

_____

"Believe. You're halfway there."

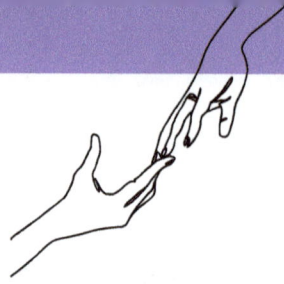

Morning Thoughts

Date: _____

Today I want to feel...

_____

_____

_____

Today I will spread kindness by...

_____

_____

_____

3 things I'm grateful for today are...

_____

_____

_____

"Happiness is a habit."

Evening Thoughts

3 things I'm grateful for today are...

_____

_____

_____

The best part of today was...

_____

_____

_____

What can I learn from today's experiences?

_____

_____

_____

Tomorrow I'm looking forward to...

_____

_____

_____

"Do more of what you love."

Things I'm proud of achieving today are...

_____

_____

_____

_____

_____

_____

_____

_____

_____

_____

_____

_____

_____

_____

_____

"Believe. You're halfway there."

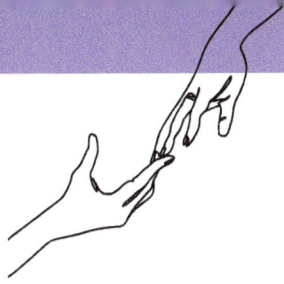

Morning Thoughts

Date: _____

Today I want to feel...

_____

_____

_____

Today I will spread kindness by...

_____

_____

_____

3 things I'm grateful for today are...

_____

_____

_____

"Happiness is a habit."

Evening Thoughts

3 things I'm grateful for today are...

_____

_____

_____

The best part of today was...

_____

_____

_____

What can I learn from today's experiences?

_____

_____

_____

Tomorrow I'm looking forward to...

_____

_____

_____

"Do more of what you love."

Things I'm proud of achieving today are...

_____

_____

_____

_____

_____

_____

_____

_____

_____

_____

_____

_____

_____

_____

"Believe. You're halfway there."

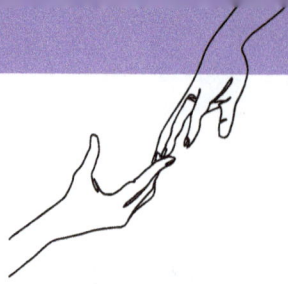

Morning Thoughts

Date: _____

Today I want to feel...

_____

_____

_____

Today I will spread kindness by...

_____

_____

_____

3 things I'm grateful for today are...

_____

_____

_____

"Happiness is a habit."

Evening Thoughts

3 things I'm grateful for today are...

_____

_____

_____

The best part of today was...

_____

_____

_____

What can I learn from today's experiences?

_____

_____

_____

Tomorrow I'm looking forward to...

_____

_____

_____

"Do more of what you love."

Things I'm proud of achieving today are...

_____

_____

_____

_____

_____

_____

_____

_____

_____

_____

_____

_____

_____

_____

_____

"Believe. You're halfway there."

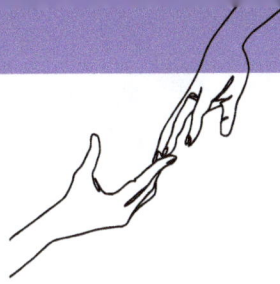

Morning Thoughts

Date: _____

Today I want to feel...

_____

_____

_____

Today I will spread kindness by...

_____

_____

_____

3 things I'm grateful for today are...

_____

_____

_____

"Happiness is a habit."

Evening Thoughts

3 things I'm grateful for today are...

_____

_____

_____

The best part of today was...

_____

_____

_____

What can I learn from today's experiences?

_____

_____

_____

Tomorrow I'm looking forward to...

_____

_____

_____

"Do more of what you love."

Things I'm proud of achieving today are...

_____

_____

_____

_____

_____

_____

_____

_____

_____

_____

_____

_____

_____

_____

"Believe. You're halfway there."

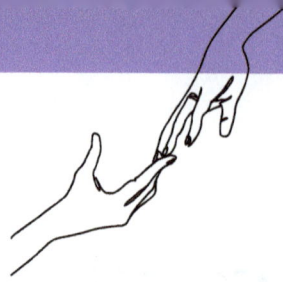

Morning Thoughts

Date: _____

Today I want to feel...

_____

_____

_____

Today I will spread kindness by...

_____

_____

_____

3 things I'm grateful for today are...

_____

_____

_____

"Happiness is a habit."

Evening Thoughts

3 things I'm grateful for today are...

_____

_____

_____

The best part of today was...

_____

_____

_____

What can I learn from today's experiences?

_____

_____

_____

Tomorrow I'm looking forward to...

_____

_____

_____

"Do more of what you love."

Things I'm proud of achieving today are...

_____

_____

_____

_____

_____

_____

_____

_____

_____

_____

_____

_____

_____

_____

_____

"Believe. You're halfway there."

Morning Thoughts

Date: _____

Today I want to feel...

_____

_____

_____

Today I will spread kindness by...

_____

_____

_____

3 things I'm grateful for today are...

_____

_____

_____

"Happiness is a habit."

Evening Thoughts

3 things I'm grateful for today are...

_____

_____

_____

The best part of today was...

_____

_____

_____

What can I learn from today's experiences?

_____

_____

_____

Tomorrow I'm looking forward to...

_____

_____

_____

"Do more of what you love."

Things I'm proud of achieving today are...

_____

_____

_____

_____

_____

_____

_____

_____

_____

_____

_____

_____

_____

_____

"Believe. You're halfway there."

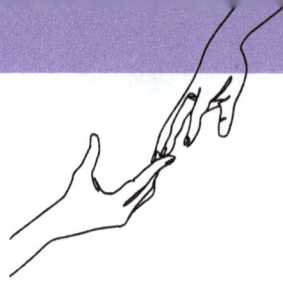

Morning Thoughts

Date: _____

Today I want to feel...

_____

_____

_____

Today I will spread kindness by...

_____

_____

_____

3 things I'm grateful for today are...

_____

_____

_____

"Happiness is a habit."

Evening Thoughts

3 things I'm grateful for today are...

_____

_____

_____

The best part of today was...

_____

_____

_____

What can I learn from today's experiences?

_____

_____

_____

Tomorrow I'm looking forward to...

_____

_____

_____

"Do more of what you love."

Things I'm proud of achieving today are...

_____

_____

_____

_____

_____

_____

_____

_____

_____

_____

_____

_____

_____

_____

"Believe. You're halfway there."

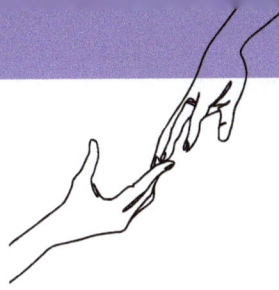

Morning Thoughts

Date: _____

Today I want to feel...

_____

_____

_____

Today I will spread kindness by...

_____

_____

_____

3 things I'm grateful for today are...

_____

_____

_____

"Happiness is a habit."

Evening Thoughts

3 things I'm grateful for today are...

_____

_____

_____

The best part of today was...

_____

_____

_____

What can I learn from today's experiences?

_____

_____

_____

Tomorrow I'm looking forward to...

_____

_____

_____

"Do more of what you love."

Things I'm proud of achieving today are...

_____

_____

_____

_____

_____

_____

_____

_____

_____

_____

_____

_____

_____

"Believe. You're halfway there."

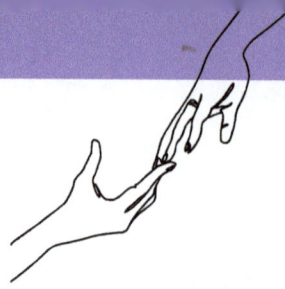

Morning Thoughts

Date: _____

Today I want to feel...

_____

_____

_____

Today I will spread kindness by...

_____

_____

_____

3 things I'm grateful for today are...

_____

_____

_____

"Happiness is a habit."

Evening Thoughts

3 things I'm grateful for today are...

_____

_____

_____

The best part of today was...

_____

_____

_____

What can I learn from today's experiences?

_____

_____

_____

Tomorrow I'm looking forward to...

_____

_____

_____

"Do more of what you love."

Things I'm proud of achieving today are...

_____

_____

_____

_____

_____

_____

_____

_____

_____

_____

_____

_____

_____

_____

"Believe. You're halfway there."

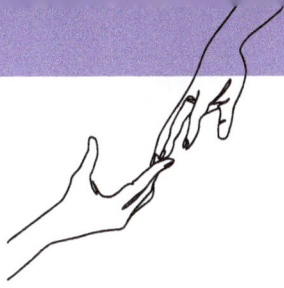

Morning Thoughts

Date: _____

Today I want to feel...

_____

_____

_____

Today I will spread kindness by...

_____

_____

_____

3 things I'm grateful for today are...

_____

_____

_____

"Happiness is a habit."

Evening Thoughts

3 things I'm grateful for today are...

_____

_____

_____

The best part of today was...

_____

_____

_____

What can I learn from today's experiences?

_____

_____

_____

Tomorrow I'm looking forward to...

_____

_____

_____

"Do more of what you love."

Things I'm proud of achieving today are...

_____

_____

_____

_____

_____

_____

_____

_____

_____

_____

_____

_____

_____

"Believe. You're halfway there."

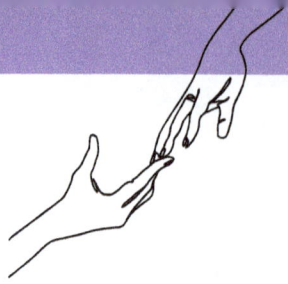

Morning Thoughts

Date: _____

Today I want to feel...

_____

_____

_____

Today I will spread kindness by...

_____

_____

_____

3 things I'm grateful for today are...

_____

_____

_____

"Happiness is a habit."

Evening Thoughts

3 things I'm grateful for today are...

_____

_____

_____

The best part of today was...

_____

_____

_____

What can I learn from today's experiences?

_____

_____

_____

Tomorrow I'm looking forward to...

_____

_____

_____

"Do more of what you love."

Things I'm proud of achieving today are...

_____

_____

_____

_____

_____

_____

_____

_____

_____

_____

_____

_____

_____

_____

"Believe. You're halfway there."

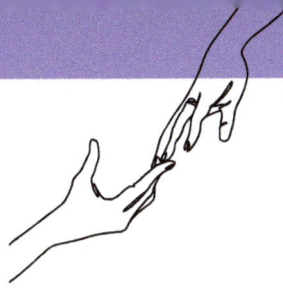

Morning Thoughts

Date: _____

Today I want to feel...

_____

_____

_____

Today I will spread kindness by...

_____

_____

_____

3 things I'm grateful for today are...

_____

_____

_____

"Happiness is a habit."

Evening Thoughts

3 things I'm grateful for today are...

_____

_____

_____

The best part of today was...

_____

_____

_____

What can I learn from today's experiences?

_____

_____

_____

Tomorrow I'm looking forward to...

_____

_____

_____

"Do more of what you love."

Things I'm proud of achieving today are...

_____

_____

_____

_____

_____

_____

_____

_____

_____

_____

_____

_____

_____

_____

"Believe. You're halfway there."

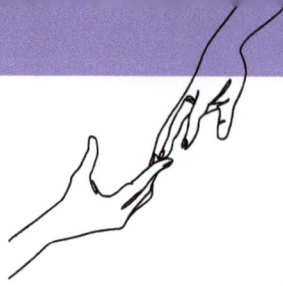

Morning Thoughts

Date: _____

Today I want to feel...

_____
_____
_____

Today I will spread kindness by...

_____
_____
_____

3 things I'm grateful for today are...

_____
_____
_____

"Happiness is a habit."

Evening Thoughts

3 things I'm grateful for today are...

_____

_____

_____

The best part of today was...

_____

_____

_____

What can I learn from today's experiences?

_____

_____

_____

Tomorrow I'm looking forward to...

_____

_____

_____

"Do more of what you love."

Things I'm proud of achieving today are...

_____

_____

_____

_____

_____

_____

_____

_____

_____

_____

_____

_____

_____

_____

"Believe. You're halfway there."

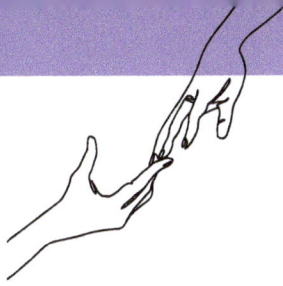

Morning Thoughts

Date: _____

Today I want to feel...

_____

_____

_____

Today I will spread kindness by...

_____

_____

_____

3 things I'm grateful for today are...

_____

_____

_____

"Happiness is a habit."

Evening Thoughts

3 things I'm grateful for today are...

_____

_____

_____

The best part of today was...

_____

_____

_____

What can I learn from today's experiences?

_____

_____

_____

Tomorrow I'm looking forward to...

_____

_____

_____

"Do more of what you love."

Things I'm proud of achieving today are...

_____

_____

_____

_____

_____

_____

_____

_____

_____

_____

_____

_____

_____

_____

"Believe. You're halfway there."

Morning Thoughts

Date: _____

Today I want to feel...

_____

_____

_____

Today I will spread kindness by...

_____

_____

_____

3 things I'm grateful for today are...

_____

_____

_____

"Happiness is a habit."

Evening Thoughts

3 things I'm grateful for today are...

_____

_____

_____

The best part of today was...

_____

_____

_____

What can I learn from today's experiences?

_____

_____

_____

Tomorrow I'm looking forward to...

_____

_____

_____

"Do more of what you love."

Things I'm proud of achieving today are...

_____

_____

_____

_____

_____

_____

_____

_____

_____

_____

_____

_____

_____

"Believe. You're halfway there."

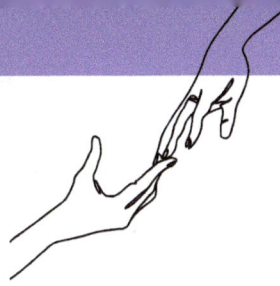

Morning Thoughts

Date: _____

Today I want to feel...

_____

_____

_____

Today I will spread kindness by...

_____

_____

_____

3 things I'm grateful for today are...

_____

_____

_____

"Happiness is a habit."

Evening Thoughts

3 things I'm grateful for today are...

_____

_____

_____

The best part of today was...

_____

_____

_____

What can I learn from today's experiences?

_____

_____

_____

Tomorrow I'm looking forward to...

_____

_____

_____

"Do more of what you love."

Evening Thoughts

3 things I'm grateful for today are...

_____

_____

_____

The best part of today was...

_____

_____

_____

What can I learn from today's experiences?

_____

_____

_____

Tomorrow I'm looking forward to...

_____

_____

_____

"Do more of what you love."

Things I'm proud of achieving today are...

_____

_____

_____

_____

_____

_____

_____

_____

_____

_____

_____

_____

_____

_____

"Believe. You're halfway there."

You made it!

Congratulations on reaching the last page of this journal and on seeking your purpose throughout these pages! These past thirty days have been a journey, but it is a journey that does not end with the closing of this book. The next step, and the most important on this path of self-discovery, is to hold tight to what you have learned across these pages and carry it with you along the ongoing journey of your life.

Hold your passion high and wear it well as you walk with purpose into each new day. Good luck, and never forget that your passion and your purpose have been within you all along.

-Purp

www.ingramcontent.com/pod-product-compliance
Lightning Source LLC
Chambersburg PA
CBHW052117020426

42335CB00021B/2799